CLEVELAND RADIO PLAYERS

Published by Cleveland Radio Players

ISBN 978-0692370469 (Cleveland Radio Players, The)

Original adaption and Performances

Originally adapted for the radio and performed by The Cleveland Radio Players. Directed by Milton Matthew Horowitz. Recorded at Bad Racket Studios. Theme song music "The Idealist" by Sridharan Ravichandran.

Starring:

Denny Castiglione	Narrator
Jack Matuszewski	Cameron
Deanna Dionne	Marie
Cory Shy	Bain
Kat Bi	Deitrich
Robert Branch	President, Anya's Mother
Llenelle Gibson	Anya
David Flynt	J.C.

Phoenix
The Radio Play

Written By Scott Fivelson

Directed by Milton Horowitz

theradioplayers@gmail.com

2218 Superior Ave suite #203
Cleveland Ohio 44114

216 269 4171

CAST OF CHARACTERS

Cameron: An immunologist.

Marie: An epidemiologist.

Dietrich: A infectious disease physician.

J.C.: A laboratory tech.

Anya: A laboratory tech.

Bain: A government agent.

Anya's Mother: A dream figure.

The President: A world leader.

PHOENIX OPENING CREDITS

ROLL IN OPENING FAN FARE

NARRATOR
Greetings and salutations... You're listening to THE CLEVELAND RADIO PLAYERS performance of PHOENIX - a one-act thriller by SCOTT FIVELSON, directed by MILTON HOROWITZ, narrated by DENNIS CASTIGLIONE.

SCENE 1

MUSIC: "THE IDEALIST" MUSIC SECTION 1

NARRATOR
Scene one... Location... An underground laboratory... Somewhere in the state of Arizona.

NARRATOR
Time... The near future... Deep underground echoes the sound of fitful and TROUBLED MOANS.

ROLL IN "UNDERGROUND LAB" ENVIRONMENT

FADE OUT MUSIC

ANYA MOANS

(CONTINUED)

NARRATOR
A blond woman in her 20's. Curled up on her cot, she looks pale, fragile. She is asleep and dreaming. She suffers in her sleep. WHIMPERING in fear.

ANYA WHIMPERS

ANYA
No... (beat) Mother, no...

NARRATOR
A vision of ANYA'S MOTHER appears. In her hospital gown, she is a ghostly wraith, and has been bleeding from her eyes and nose... She advances slowly toward the girl as she dreams...

GHOSTLY SWELL

ANYA'S MOTHER
Anya... Why didn't you help me?... Anya...

ANYA
No!

NARRATOR
Another woman rushes to Anya's side.

FAST FEMALE FOOTSTEPS

Older than Anya, but much younger than her mother... 30... smart as a whip... DIETRICH. She wears a lab coat.

DIETRICH
It's okay... You're having a dream ...

THRASHING SFX

NARRATOR
She holds Anya as the girl thrashes.

DIETRICH
It's just a dream state... It's alright.

NARRATOR
Anya looks up, wild-eyed.

ANYA
No - it's not.

NARRATOR
Anya's very much awake. Dietrich meets her gaze.

MUSIC CUE: 80'S HOLIDAY SONG

NARRATOR
J.C. -- a lab technician, African-American, late 20's -- walks along with a clip board of data and a pen, making notations as he checks on the latest series of results. He is in the main laboratory of a secure underground bunker, indeed, somewhere in Arizona. So deep in the ground, it feels closer to China. He listens to music on a latest generation iPod.

J.C.
(singing)
celebrate.... holiday....

NARRATOR
He is undeniably grooving to the music, when enters his boss.

SHORT FOOTSTEPS

NARRATOR
MARIE, 32, an epidemiologist, earnest and dedicated. Her resistant exterior often camouflages the fact that she has more heart than is perhaps prudent for someone in her position. J.C. doesn't know he's being watched.

J.C.
(singing)
It would be reeeeal nice...

NARRATOR
Marie marches up from behind, and like the good angel on his shoulder--

MARIE CLEARS HER THROAT

MUSIC STOPS ABRUPTLY

NARRATOR
Catching him a bit off-guard, J.C. quickly pockets the earpiece.

SCRIBBLING

J.C.
(beat)
Just following protocols, ma'am. Recording the data.

MARIE
I can see that.

NARRATOR
He gives her a glance. Jots down more results.

SCRIBBLING

MARIE
Can I see those numbers?

J.C.
Knock yourself out.

NARRATOR
Marie looks over the data. Any levity leaves her face.

MARIE
Still hemorrhagic.

J.C.
Looks that way, don't it... Just like every other day.

NARRATOR
Marie hands back the data. J.C. resumes his strolling clipboard vigil. He stops.

FOOTSTEPS STOPPING

J.C.
We gonna win this one, Doc?...

MARIE
Of course we are.

J.C.
'Cause I see these results. And I ain't feelin' the love. (beat) I ain't the only one. Coupla nights ago, me and Anya, we're talkin'. "So Anya," I say to her, "when we get outta this sinkhole, who you gonna marry - Brad Pitt or George Clooney?" She says, "George Clooney's dead... John Mayer's dead... They're all dead."

MARIE
We don't know that.

J.C.
Don't know about the TV in your penthouse, Doc, but all I get is static.

NARRATOR
J.C. stares at Marie hard. This is a frightened man.

J.C.
We don't know the toll it's taken. Hell, we don't even know what we're fightin'. Bird flu? With proteins that walk the walk like Ebola? Mama didn't raise no vaccination pincushion... don't-add-up is all I'm sayin'.

MARIE
I guess she didn't.

NARRATOR
Marie thinks about it - and decides to tell J.C.

MARIE
We know what we're fighting...

J.C.
Hmm?...

MARIE
We know what we're fighting. Cameron and I.

J.C
And you ain't thought to tell your ol' buddy J.C.?... Now you're pissin' me off, Doc.

MARIE
J.C. - doesn't have Q clearance.

NARRATOR
He actually accepts that explanation. However, today, that degree of disclosure is not enough for Marie.

MARIE
Okay, look. You just got an upgrade. (lowers her voice) The pandemic we have been battling is not bird flu. Nor is it Marburg. Nor is it anything off the menu of the gnarliest super-viruses on earth.

J.C.
You're scarin' me, Doc.

MARIE
You were already scared.

J.C.
It was created in a lab, wasn't it? (almost gleeful) I knew it.

MARIE
If it was - not around here. ...

J.C.
(gleeful) Aliens! ... I knew it!

NARRATOR
With J.C. still in the cheerful afterglow of revelation, and conspiracy-theory confirmed, into the lab walks BAIN...

SLOW MALE FOOTSTEPS

Bain is in his 30's, isotope serious, sport coat and tie... and somewhere under that coat, a sidearm that takes 14 in the clip and one in the pipe... No one's friend... There by the good graces of some undisclosed agency with an

(MORE)

NARRATOR (cont'd)
acronym. J.C. doesn't much care for Bain. So he walks.

FOOTSTEPS WALKING AWAY

The moment J.C. is gone--

BAIN
Any problem, ma'am?

MARIE
No, no problem.

NARRATOR
Still hitting her with that thousand-yard stare when enters CAMERON.

SINGLE MALE FOOTSTEPS

Not yet 40, and already the leading immunologist in the hemisphere... already showing the wear and tear of years fighting for the CDC, yet still resembles the freewheeling, Pentagon-shunning MIT wunderkind he once was. Not surprisingly, despite the help of his research partner Marie... who also happens to be his wife... he's still not quite housebroken. Cameron throws a stare right back at Bain.

CAMERON
Hey, sport - in case you haven't actually noticed - we're in the middle of a global pandemic, it's an Earth-killer, and my people work best without a German Shepherd sniffin' around their rim... You got something to secure? Why don'tcha go secure it.

NARRATOR
Bain, often a man of few words, sneers sarcastically, and walks off.

FOOTSTEPS AWAY

CAMERON
Somebody oughta tell him that men and women with high levels of hostility often show high levels of
(MORE)

CAMERON (cont'd)
homocysteine - and that can lead to heart disease... poor fella.

NARRATOR
Marie loves Cameron when he's brilliant.

CAMERON
(thoughtfully) Of course, like my favorite windbreaker, everything's potentially reversible...

MARIE
I thought I threw that one out.

CAMERON
My theory?

MARIE
Your windbreaker.

NARRATOR
Cameron flashes a crooked smile.

CAMERON
I rescued it... Just like I'm gonna save us, Marie.

NARRATOR
She'd like to believe it... She's got to believe it... She DOES believe it.

MARIE
When this is all over, I've gotta take you shopping.

CAMERON
(sweetly) Alright.

MARIE:
Now I know it's the end of the world. First, they give us grant money, and now you're willing to go shopping.

CAMERON
I just wish we had more time...

MARIE
I told J.C. what we're doing here.

CAMERON
(cross) Marie.

MARIE
At least started to.

CAMERON:
That's why Bain was nervous... Of course, he'll feel better after he's had his morning coffee and beaten a confession out of one of the chimps... Still... this is classified stuff, darlin'.

MARIE
J.C. has a right to know. They all do.

CAMERON
How's it gonna help them do their admittedly invaluable, but ultimately, call it grunt work, to know that patient zero was an alien astronaut who was found dead at a crash site by Old MacDonald who had a farm, ee-i-ee-i-o?

NARRATOR
Dietrich strolls in.

SHORT FEMALE FOOTSTEPS

DIETRICH
You don't wanna tell Anya.

NARRATOR
Now Dietrich knows too.

CAMERON
Great. Why don't we just post it in the mess hall.

DIETRICH
We're livin' in pretty tight quarters, Cam.

NARRATOR
Marie is relieved at the security breach.

MARIE
I'm sorry, Dietrich.

DIETRICH:
I'm not sweatin' it. We've got a job to do.

MARIE
Maybe Anya ought to know.

DIETRICH
You don't want that kinda pain.

CAMERON
We'll have to ship her out.

MARIE
Where to?

FADE OUT ENVIRONMENT

MUSIC CUE: "THE IDEALIST" SECTION 2

ANYA SUFFERING IN HER SLEEP

SCENE 2

NARRATOR
Scene two... Anya is curled up on her cot, asleep and dreaming...

FADE OUT "THE IDEALIST"

ROLL IN "UNDERGROUND LAB" ENVIRONMENT

ANYA MOANS

NARRATOR
She MOANS FEARFULLY.

INCOMING VIDEO TRANSMISSION

CAMERON
(his voice in the dark) Mr. President?

NARRATOR
Anya is still tossing and turning, Cameron is seated in front of his laptop...

PRESIDENT
Hello Cameron.

NARRATOR
The PRESIDENT, suited and presidential, is a bit of a surrealistic presence... For the President is not present... he is being broadcast by a video feed.

NARRATOR
From his first words, he is confident and inspiring.

PRESIDENT
How are you holding up down there?

CAMERON
We're fine, Mr. President.

PRESIDENT
And how's Marie?

CAMERON
Everyone's fine, sir. Thank you for asking.

PRESIDENT
These are dark days, Cameron. For America... For the world... But I know that we both believe that, by rising to the occasion, like so many generations of Americans before us, we can rise up out of this darkness. (beat) How is the serum progressing?

CAMERON
We're getting there, Mr. President. As you know, it is a much broader spectrum vaccine than the one we originally envisioned. Running a real risk of failure.

PRESIDENT
Off-set by the limitless potential rewards.

CAMERON
(can't help smiling) Yes.

ANYA MOANS AGAIN IN HER SLEEP

PRESIDENT
This is your baby, Cameron... If it works, this nation ... this world
(MORE)

PRESIDENT (cont'd)
... will owe you a great debt of gratitude.

CAMERON
Like you've said, sir... out of this tragedy, humanity has been presented with an opportunity.

PRESIDENT
The Vice-President, the Speaker of the House, the whole inner circle ... they're all excited.

CAMERON
And how's everyone doing down there?

PRESIDENT
Of course, we're quite well-supplied here. Some of my staff have taken to calling it Camp Goliath... I'm not sure how I feel about that.
(A DRY CHUCKLE. Then, with serious import--)
Tens of millions are dying each week, from the deadliest scourge we've ever seen... Perhaps God Almighty did send this super-virus for a reason... Does your bunker have a chapel?

CAMERON
No, Mr. President.

PRESIDENT
It should. (beat) Keep me in the loop.

END VIDEO TRANSMISSION

FADE OUT ENVIRONMENT

MUSIC CUE: "THE IDEALIST" SECTION 3

SCENE 3

NARRATOR
Scene three...

FADE OUT MUSIC

(CONTINUED)

ROLL IN "UNDERGROUND LAB" ENVIRONMENT

ANYA
We're not gonna die!... We're not gonna die!...

NARRATOR
Anya, on her cot, is hysterical.

LONG THRASHING SOUNDS

J.C. and Marie struggle to restrain her, while Dietrich advances on her with a hypodermic needle.

DIETRICH
Hold her steady!

MARIE
No, we're not gonna die...

J.C.
It's alright, it's gonna be alright...

NARRATOR
Bain watches from the corner of the room, his sport coat pushed aside - his hand on his sidearm. At the ready to be heavy backup.

ANYA
No, no, no - no sleep. I don't wanna sleep... Please...

NARRATOR
Dietrich hits her with the needle.

SOUND OF INJECTION

NARRATOR
J.C. ever-so-gently brushes the hair away from Anya's beautiful, tortured face. The sedative takes quick effect, and they're able to release her as she loses consciousness. As the dust settles...

BAIN
You don't have time for this.

DIETRICH
Bain's right... Can you mind her? I've got some results I need to double-check that are not making any sense to me at all.

MARIE
We're fine here.

NARRATOR
Mainly because Marie's holding it together. Dietrich walks out, looking determined.

FEMALE FOOTSTEPS AWAY

BAIN
No time for this at all.

MALE FOOTSTEPS AWAY

NARRATOR
Bain follows after Dietrich.

Marie surveys Anya, in her quiet, sedated sleep. Then looks to J.C.

MARIE
What happened?

J.C.
The poor girl, woke up screamin'.

MARIE
She dreams about her mother.

J.C.
I know. But not this time, not this one... I sincerely wish your better half would speed up the cure... Anya ain't so crazy... Everyone at Homeland is dead... Everyone at the CDC is dead... She called it.

RISING TENSION

NARRATOR
Both peer down at Anya, like she's the sleeping oracle.

MARIE
What is it that you see in your dreams?

NARRATOR
Anya's eyes pop open.

ANYA
Ask Cameron.

CINEMATIC SWISH

FADE OUT ENVIRONMENT

MUSIC CUE: "THE IDEALIST" SECTION 4

SCENE 4

NARRATOR
Scene four.

FADE OUT MUSIC

ROLL IN "UNDERGROUND LAB" ENVIRONMENT

NARRATOR
A transmission from the President begins on a video feed.

START VIDEO FEED

PRESIDENT
I'm sorry we had to keep you in the dark for so long, Marie... That was my call... I felt that Cameron needed total and unwavering support.

NARRATOR
Cameron is seated at his laptop, Marie behind him, with a hand on his shoulder.

MARIE
(shaky)... I support Cameron in anything he does, end of story.

NARRATOR
True as that may be, her voice is undeniably shaky. The President has the good grace not to comment on it.

PRESIDENT
I'm glad to hear you say that, Marie... Because we've reached a
(MORE)

PRESIDENT (cont'd)
juncture where Cameron has never needed you more... The project has never needed you more.

MARIE
I hadn't meant to doubt, Mr. President.

NARRATOR
The President raises a strong open hand, as he might in making a heartfelt point while addressing the nation.

PRESIDENT
We've all had doubts. We who have known that there exists only one of two choices ... use the very rare blood and organs harvested from the being found at the crash site to create a vaccine that might eradicate this plague ... or a vaccine that might let us live forever. (beat)

MARIE
It is hard to believe, Mr. President.

CAMERON
Let him finish--

PRESIDENT
Cameron believes - and I, for one, believe with him - that we finally have the materials at hand to create an alternate serum that could trigger an immune response beyond modern science's wildest dreams.

NARRATOR
The prospect of this makes the President almost giddy.

PRESIDENT
An anti-aging, regenerative healing ability... A Superman pill!

CAMERON
Don't say that... (catches himself) It's an injection, sir.

PRESIDENT
One that bestows immortality.

NARRATOR
The President falls silent, almost humbled at the prospect.

MARIE
But haven't you yourself said that this alien's blood SHOULD yield an antidote to this virus? While this other research carries with it the extremely high risk that--

PRESIDENT
That we're chasing a chimera? Yes, we could fail. And go down fighting, Marie. But it's ten seconds to midnight on the Doomsday Clock. I don't intend to let that clock strike twelve under my administration.

MARIE
You know we'll do our best, Mr. President.

PRESIDENT
That's all I wanted to hear. (beat) I'll tell the Cabinet.

NARRATOR
A thin and appreciative smile for a job well done. And end of transmission.

END VIDEO FEED

NARRATOR
Cameron puts his hand on Marie's.

CAMERON
Always said I'd love ya forever, baby.

HIGH HEEL FOOTSTEPS AWAY

NARRATOR
Marie walks out of the lab, leaving Cameron sitting alone.

FADE OUT ENVIRONMENT

FADE IN

MUSIC CUE: "THE IDEALIST" SECTION 5

SCENE 5

NARRATOR
Scene five.

FADE OUT MUSIC

ROLL IN "UNDERGROUND LAB" ENVIRONMENT

BAIN
(hard as nails) Sit... down!

SUSPENDED TENSION

NARRATOR
In another room in this underground facility, Cameron is seated. Marie anxiously backs into the chair beside him, at gunpoint. Bain is in a one-handed combat stance. Wanting some answers.

BAIN
(hotly) We have been stationed here with one objective only: To find a cure. IS THAT YOUR INTENTION?... I repeat: IS THAT YOUR INTENTION?

NARRATOR
Cameron and Marie can't help but be rattled by Bain's hyper-aggressiveness. Marie, though, more than Cameron.

MARIE
Of course--Of course, it is.

CAMERON
Just put down the weapon, Bain.

NARRATOR
He doesn't.

BAIN
Cameron... Tonight, at approximately o-six-hundred, I dropped a laboratory rat in a pot of boiling water.

CAMERON
(slow and sarcastic) You sick son-of-a--

BAIN
By o-seven-hundred, the animal's third-degree burns were gone... By o-eight-hundred, it's dead. (beat) What's going on? (beat)

CAMERON
That's what you call empirical research, Marie.

NARRATOR
Incredibly brazen in the face of that .45 caliber.

BAIN
We have a mission.

CAMERON
Yes, we do.

BAIN
Just wanted to know if we're on the same page.

NARRATOR
Marie glances at Cameron.

CAMERON
I thought you were the President's boy.

NARRATOR
Bain looks awfully tempted to put down that gun, and kick Cameron's wunderkind face.

BAIN
I'm in communication with the President... But not on all matters, apparently.

NARRATOR
Marie's got to speak up here.

MARIE
Bain. I want you to know that when I first heard of the revised medical protocol, I had huge reservations.

BAIN
And you're gonna tell me all about it.

NARRATOR
Reminding Marie that he's still the man with the gun.

BAIN
Talk, Marie.

CAMERON
It's alright... Go ahead, he serves the President.

BAIN
Wrong... ... I did serve the President... now I serve three hundred million dead Americans.

CAMERON
What if you could beat death?... Not just the virus, not just cancer ... but the whole damn human condition?

NARRATOR
As close to invulnerable as Bain is, he very nearly flinches at the onslaught of questions.

CAMERON
What if you could?

NARRATOR
Gun still trained on them, Bain flinches when the ALARM SOUNDS.

ALARM SOUND CUT IN

NARRATOR
Cameron's actually the first to react, already out of his seat.

CAMERON
Did somebody order frickin' take-out?

NARRATOR
Bain's gun is still at the ready, but no longer ready to use on them.

BAIN
Or there's been a breach.

MEN RUNNING FOOTSTEPS

WOMAN RUNNING FOOTSTEPS

NARRATOR
The two men and Marie run down the hall and into the room where a video feed is in progress -- via the security camera at ground level outside the installation. What they see is J.C., looking abject and fearful, standing outside the airlocked door, peering over his shoulder anxiously.

CUT OUT RUNNING SOUNDS

BANGING ON DOOR 1

J.C.
Cameron - let me back in, man... Let me back in...

BANGING ON DOOR 2

NARRATOR
Cameron is right there behind his laptop, Marie at his side. Anya is beside herself with worry, positively freaking out. Bain and Dietrich attempt to restrain her.

CAMERON
I can't do it, buddy... Why'd you go out there? (aside) He's infected... Gotta be...

ANYA
J.C. - just hold on, baby! (aside) What're you waiting for?? LET 'IM BACK IN!!

DIETRICH
Will somebody please--

NARRATOR
Marie slaps her hand down on a console button and the ALARM CEASES.

BUTTON SLAP

CUT OUT ALARM SOUND

NARRATOR
The accompanying human sense of high alarm and distress remains.

J.C.
Cameron... seriously. I ain't gonna make you guys sick. I ain't been out here a moment.

CAMERON
Does anybody know--

ANYA
He knows I don't wanna take the serum. He went outside to prove that everything's alright.

J.C.
It's not alright. They're droppin' like flies, man. You gotta get my ass inside now! Sweet Jesus, it's me. I'm your friend! Best man at your wedding!

NARRATOR
Bain fast-draws his weapon and trains it on Cameron, as Dietrich holds writhing Anya.

BAIN
Don't you do it.

CAMERON
Just calm down, J.C.

J.C.
I don't wanna die out here, Cameron...

(CONTINUED)

CONTINUED:

DIETRICH
I hate to say it, but he made his choice. We've got to stay in lockdown.

NARRATOR
Marie puts a strong hand on Cameron's arm. He looks at her.(beat)

MARIE
What if that were me?

NARRATOR
Cameron just looks at Marie, then back at the video feed.

J.C.
Cameron...

MARIE
What if that were me?

NARRATOR
Bain almost doesn't know who to aim at, Cameron or Marie.

BAIN
DON'T DO IT!

BAIN COCKS GUN

NARRATOR
Cameron turns to face the muzzle of Bain's gun.

CAMERON
That IS me.

NARRATOR
Swiveling back, he slaps the other button on the console, the one that permits entry. The ALARM SOUNDS AGAIN.

BUTTON SLAP

AIRLOCK

ALARM SOUND CUT IN

(CONTINUED)

ANYA
Thank you--!

NARRATOR
J.C. ducks inside... Bain can not
shoot...

ALARM SOUND FADES OUT

FADE OUT ENVIRONMENT

MUSIC CUE: "THE IDEALIST" SECTION 6

SCENE 6

NARRATOR
Scene six.

FADE OUT MUSIC

ROLL IN "UNDERGROUND LAB" ENVIRONMENT

NARRATOR
The lab is dark. All that can be
heard is SHIVERING, ABSOLUTE
SHIVERING.

SOUNDS OF SHIVERING

NARRATOR
Marie, blanket wrapped around
herself, hunched on her cot.
Dietrich beside her, seeking to
comfort her.

MARIE
Cold... (beat) I'm-I'm cold...

SHIVERING

NARRATOR
Even though she's drenched in
sweat.

DIETRICH
I know... I know. (beat)

START VIDEO TRANSMISSION

PRESIDENT
(firmly) Cameron.

NARRATOR
Cameron, at his laptop.

PRESIDENT
I cannot deny that I'm very disturbed by what I'm hearing... I still don't understand how you allowed this so-called breach to take place.

CAMERON
Mr. President--

PRESIDENT
(uncharacteristically ill-tempered)
Did you send somebody out to walk the dog? The Earth's turning into a bio-graveyard, son. It's supposed to be your job to stop it... Where's Marie?

CAMERON
I was trying to tell you, Mr. President. She's very sick.

NARRATOR
The President is visibly shaken by this. Processing it all quickly, he strives to switch gears to his trademark penchant for warmth and connection.

PRESIDENT
Please extend to your wife my very best wishes for a speedy recovery. Because a serum is coming - correct? Is anyone else infected? You're leading the research. How are you feeling?

NARRATOR
Cameron, who has been masking his emotions to an impressive degree, can't do it any longer.

CAMERON
Like my wife is dying, sir. And like it's not too late to change paths. (beat) We've known since the crash and the harvest that we would have limited materials from which to manufacture an effective antibiotic... But we also know - we
(MORE)

CAMERON (cont'd)
think we know - that a cure for the virus... it's do-able.

PRESIDENT
You think you know... I'm sorry, Cameron... that's just not going to be good enough.

CAMERON
Mr. President, with respect, isn't it a helluva lot better than rolling the dice on a wing and a prayer?

PRESIDENT
Cameron, did you ever see the musical, Man of La Mancha?... When this is all over, you should see it... In the meantime, I've got to attribute it to your personal concerns that it can be hard to stay on task. But stay on task you must... (confidential) I'll let you in on a little secret... You may find this shocking. But such are the burdens of my high office...

SUSPENDED TENSION

We released the virus.

CAMERON
What?

PRESIDENT
We released the virus to lessen our numbers, since the one thing knew is that Mother Earth could never sustain our population once gifted with eternal life. So you see, at this point, not to create the full-spectrum vaccine... it would be such a waste.

CAMERON
(quietly) Yes, Mr. President.

PRESIDENT
Son, we didn't ask for this test. But now that it's here, we cannot fail to meet the challenge... When you and I look back at Mankind's darkest hour, maybe over a beer, do
(MORE)

(CONTINUED)

PRESIDENT (cont'd)
you know what you'll say to me a thousand years from now?

NARRATOR
Cameron taps a key on the laptop... and ends the transmission with the President.

END VIDEO TRANSMISSION

NARRATOR
Cameron sits there in the dark with a sense of utter desolation... Jumps up and walks out quickly.

FADE OUT ENVIRONMENT

MUSIC CUE: "THE IDEALIST" SECTION 7

SCENE 7

NARRATOR
Scene seven.

FADE OUT MUSIC

ROLL IN "UNDERGROUND LAB" ENVIRONMENT

NARRATOR
It's dark in the lab... all that can be heard is SORROWFUL SOBBING.

J.C. AND ANYA SOBBING

J.C.
(coughing)
Why'd ya do it, Anya?... Why'd ya throw OUR chances away?... We were sooo close... So close...

ANYA
(weak)
These dreams - I'll have them for the rest of my life. I'll never make it. You can't make me live forever!

NARRATOR
As their forlorn weeping begins to abate, there's almost relief--

J.C.
(dying)
Don't gotta worry about that no more...

NARRATOR
J.C. is seated on a cot holding Anya and rocking her. Both show the signs of bleeding from their eyes and noses.

FADE IN REGULAR HEART BEAT

CAMERON
I love you, Marie. I'll always love you, Marie.

IRREGULAR HEARTBEAT

FLATLINE

NARRATOR
Marie lies on a cot in Cameron's arms... She's gone...

CHARACTER DEATH

FADE OUT ENVIRONMENT

MUSIC CUE: "THE IDEALIST" SECTION 8

SCENE 8

NARRATOR
Final scene.

FADE OUT MUSIC

ROLL IN "UNDERGROUND LAB" ENVIRONMENT

BAIN
I'll go on the bullet train... oughta be there, two hours.

NARRATOR
The trio of Cameron, Bain, and Dietrich ... the survivors ... all face each other. Cameron holds a silver briefcase.

CAMERON
It's a strictly one-way ticket, you know.

NARRATOR
Bain nods, with stoical acceptance. He takes the briefcase from Cameron... ... The two men never did see eye to eye. Still, they shake hands. Bonded by, if nothing else, what they must do now. Bain walks toward the exit.

SLOW FOOTSTEPS THEN STOP

CAMERON
See ya on the other side.

BAIN
(for him, oddly wry and philosophical) We'll see.

BUTTON

AIRLOCK 1&2

NARRATOR
Bain exits the lab. Leaving the last living beings in the underground bunker... Cameron and Dietrich look at each other. They hug, fiercely. Dietrich's never cried in her life. Ain't gonna cry now. But she admits--

DIETRICH
I don't feel too well.

CAMERON
Why don't you go lie down.

DIETRICH
Ya sure?

NARRATOR
He is. Dietrich gives him a sturdy little one-handed thumb's up, as weak as she is.

DIETRICH
(coughing)
Give 'em hell.

FEMALE FOOTSTEPS FADING

NARRATOR
Dietrich exits. Cameron stands alone... ... walks to his chair, and takes his seat in front of the laptop. His voice has a calmness to it.

START VIDEO TRANSMISSION

CAMERON
Mr. President...

NARRATOR
The President is per usual on the video feed. But what's atypical is his relative breeziness in dress and demeanor. Still suited, but sans the tie... his shirt open-necked at the collar. His hair a little fluffier. Hard to put a finger on it, but he seems somehow... invigorated.

PRESIDENT
Cameron!

CAMERON
How are you, sir?

PRESIDENT
In the pink... In the pink of health, as they used to say!... After our last talk, I didn't quite know what to expect. As I told my V.P., that boy's got spunk, but a lot to learn. And it looks like you've learned it!

CAMERON
Well, I don't quite know what to say to that, Mr. President. I guess, "If you can't please everyone, well, ya - gotta please yourself." (flip beat) Ricky Nelson.

NARRATOR
Perhaps sensing some glitch, the President's still supremely buoyant.

PRESIDENT
Ya lost me there, but I love keepin' up with the kids. Keep rappin'.

CAMERON
Well, you know that vaccine you were waiting for? It seems one of my people vetoed it.

PRESIDENT
(cheery nonethless) Vetoed it?

CAMERON
Radiated the supply.

PRESIDENT
(a disbelieving CHUCKLE) That's unthinkable!

CAMERON
Guess that's what she thought.

PRESIDENT
Doesn't make any sense. Bain made it. 'Course he looks a little peaked... We've all had our injections.

CAMERON
And how is the rest of the inner circle, the whole gang at Camp Goliath?

NARRATOR
The President's just too energized to be brought down by Cameron's sarcasm, but yes, something about it is starting to ding him... Cameron's own energy... it's starting to flag.

PRESIDENT
I meant to speak to you on that subject... How long does it take for the serum to kick in?

CAMERON
They should all be dead in a day.

NARRATOR
We can tell Cameron will be too.

PRESIDENT
Don't play with me, son.

CAMERON
I ain't playin'. The die was cast. By both of us. As we've known all along, there were never enough genetic materials from the crash site to manufacture two serums... Just one... And that ship has sailed.

PRESIDENT
Then what have we just injected ourselves with?

CAMERON
The virus.

NARRATOR
A dramatic pause... ... The President is dumbfounded... Almost amused. It couldn't be true!

PRESIDENT
Since there's no cure above ground among the dead and the dying, if you've effectively pulled this stunt... you just killed off the human race!... And that's not possible. Look at me!

NARRATOR
The President's looking positively robust.

PRESIDENT
I feel like a teenager!

NARRATOR
It's getting harder and harder for Cameron to keep focused.

CAMERON
I'm sorry, Mr. President. I'm going to have to cut this short... I'm going to miss Marie.

NARRATOR
Cameron's almost in the twilight sleep that precedes the eternal one. Suddenly, he forces himself to consciousness--

CAMERON
We did manage to save one... One
dose of the immortality drug...
It's now in your system... I guess
it works... (coughing)

PRESIDENT
But-but-but what about everyone
else?

CAMERON
(coughing) Have a nice life.

NARRATOR
Power reserves go out at the lab.
Darkness falls on Cameron.

POWER DOWN SFX

CUT OUT ENVIRONMENT

NARRATOR
The President, bristling with
bottomless reserves of energy,
illuminates the laboratory from
Cameron's laptop... The President
begins to visualize his future.

PRESIDENT
Cameron...

NARRATOR
There is no reply.

PRESIDENT
Cameron!

NARRATOR
Still silence.

PRESIDENT
CAMERON!!!

END VIDEO TRANSMISSION

MUSIC CUE: "THE IDEALIST" SECTION 8

END CREDITS

OUTRO MUSIC

NARRATOR
You have been listening to THE CLEVELAND RADIO PLAYERS performance of PHOENIX, a one-act thriller by SCOTT FIVELSON, directed by MILTON HOROWITZ, narrated by DENNIS CASTIGLIONE, recorded at BAD RACKET STUDIOS... Starring:

JACK MATUSZEWSKI

DEANNA DIONNE

CORY SHY

KAT BI (BEE)

ROBERT BRANCH

LLENELLE GIBSON

DAVID FLYNT

MUSIC FADES

About The Author

Scott Fivelson is the author of the novel, *Tuxes*, the one-act plays *Dial L for Latch-Key* and *Leading the Witness*, and *Johnny Passe*, a classic in the fiction noir genre. His film, *American Reel*, starring David Carradine, Michael Maloney, and Mariel Hemingway, was recently re-released on DVD. His film, *3 Holes and a Smoking Gun*, stars James Wilder, Joaquim de Almeida, Rudolf Martin, and Richard Edson.

Rights and Royalties

Originally adapted for the radio and performed by The Cleveland Radio Players

Directed by Milton Matthew Horowitz

Recorded at Bad Racket Studios

Theme song music "The Idealist" by Sridharan Ravichandran

For more information on performance rights and royalties, or to listen to Fall Out Guys as a radio play, please visit www.ClevelandRadioPlayers.com

www.ingramcontent.com/pod-product-compliance
Lightning Source LLC
Chambersburg PA
CBHW081024040426
42444CB00014B/3343
9780692370469